ULTIMATE MANGA

HOW TO DRAW

CUTE MANGA

Marc Powell and David Neal

PowerKiDS press™

New York

WITH THANKS TO ODA, STEVE, AILIN, AND PAT

Published in 2016 by **The Rosen Publishing Group**
29 East 21st Street, New York, NY 10010

Text by Jack Hawkins
Edited by Jack Hawkins
Designed by Dynamo Ltd and Emma Randall
Cover design by Notion Design
Illustrations by Marc Powell and David Neal

Cataloging-in-Publication Data
Powell, Marc.
How to draw cute manga / by Marc Powell and David Neal.
p. cm. — (Ultimate manga)
Includes index.
ISBN 978-1-4994-1139-3 (pbk.)
ISBN 978-1-4994-1149-2 (6 pack)
ISBN 978-1-4994-1170-6 (library binding)
1. Comic books, strips, etc. — Japan — Technique — Juvenile literature.
2. Cartooning — Technique — Juvenile literature. 3. Comic strip characters —
Japan — Juvenile literature. I. Title.
NC1764.5.J3 P694 2016
741.5'1—d23

Manufactured in the United States of America
CPSIA Compliance Information: Batch WS15PK: For Further Information
contact Rosen Publishing, New York, New York at 1-800-237-9932

CONTENTS

HOW TO USE THIS BOOK

The drawings in this book have been built up in seven stages. Each stage uses lines of a different color so you can see the new layer clearly. Of course, you don't have to use different colors in your work. Use a pencil for the first four stages so you can get your drawing right before moving on to the inking and coloring stages.

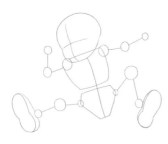

Stage 1: Green lines
This is the basic stick figure of your character.

Stage 2: Red lines
The next step is to flesh out the simple stick figure.

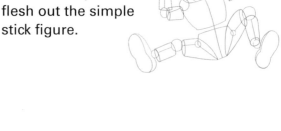

Stage 3: Blue lines
Then finish the basic shape and add in extra details.

Stage 4: Black lines
Add in clothes and any accessories.

Stage 5: Inks
The inking stage will give you a final line drawing.

Stage 6: Colors
"Flat" coloring uses lighter shades to set the base colors of your character.

Stage 7: Shading
Add shadows for light sources, and use darker colors to add depth to your character.

BASIC TOOLS

You don't need lots of complicated, expensive tools for your manga images – many of them are available from a good stationery shop. The others can be found in any art supplies store, or online.

PENCILS

These are probably the most important tool for any artist. It's important to find a type of pencil you are comfortable with, since you will be spending a lot of time using it.

Graphite

You will be accustomed to using graphite pencils – they are the familiar wood-encased "lead" pencils. They are available in a variety of densities from the softest, 9B, right up to the hardest, 9H. Hard pencils last longer and are less likely to smudge on the paper. Most artists use an HB (#2) pencil, which falls in the middle of the density scale.

Mechanical pencils

Also known as propelling pencils, these contain a length of lead that can be replaced. The leads are available in the same densities as graphite pencils. The great advantage of mechanical pencils over graphite is that you never have to sharpen them – you simply extend more lead as it wears down.

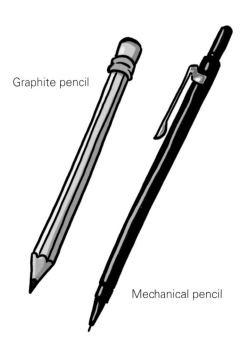

Graphite pencil

Mechanical pencil

Marker

Ballpoint pen

INKING PENS

After you have penciled your piece of artwork, you will need to ink the line to give a sharp, solid image.

Ballpoint pens

Standard ballpoint pens are ideal for lining your piece. However, their quality varies, as does their delivery of ink. A single good-quality ballpoint pen is better than a collection of cheap ones.

Marker pens

Standard marker pens of varying thicknesses are ideal for coloring and shading your artworks. They provide a steady, consistent supply of ink, and can be used to build layers of color by re-inking the same area. They are the tools most frequently used for manga coloring.

KIGURUMI KID

Kigurumi is the Japanese word for dressing in an animal suit. It can look incredibly cute, particularly on a young child. Try drawing one of your manga characters kigurumi-style – costumes based on mice, foxes, and cats all work well.

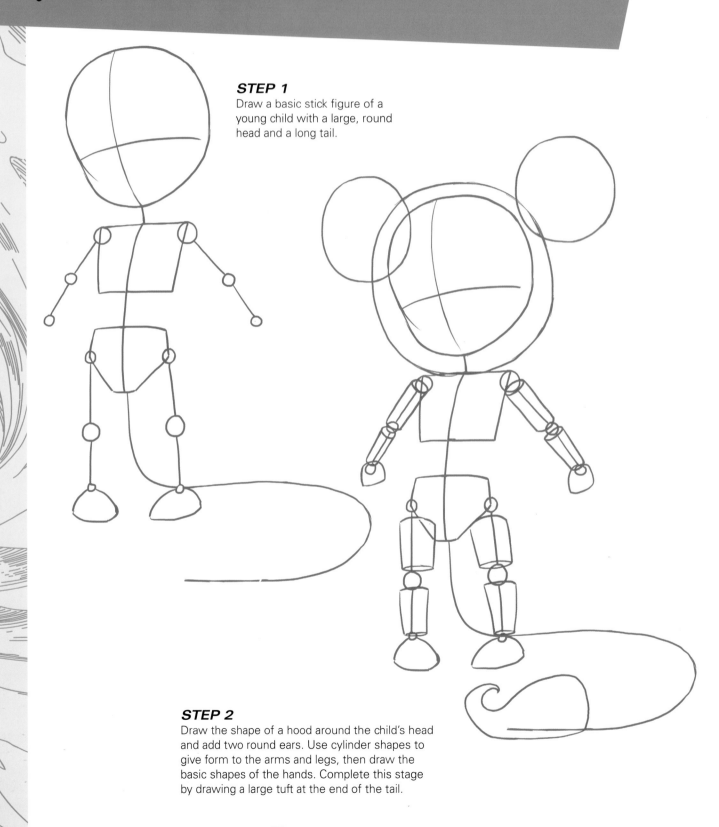

STEP 1

Draw a basic stick figure of a young child with a large, round head and a long tail.

STEP 2

Draw the shape of a hood around the child's head and add two round ears. Use cylinder shapes to give form to the arms and legs, then draw the basic shapes of the hands. Complete this stage by drawing a large tuft at the end of the tail.

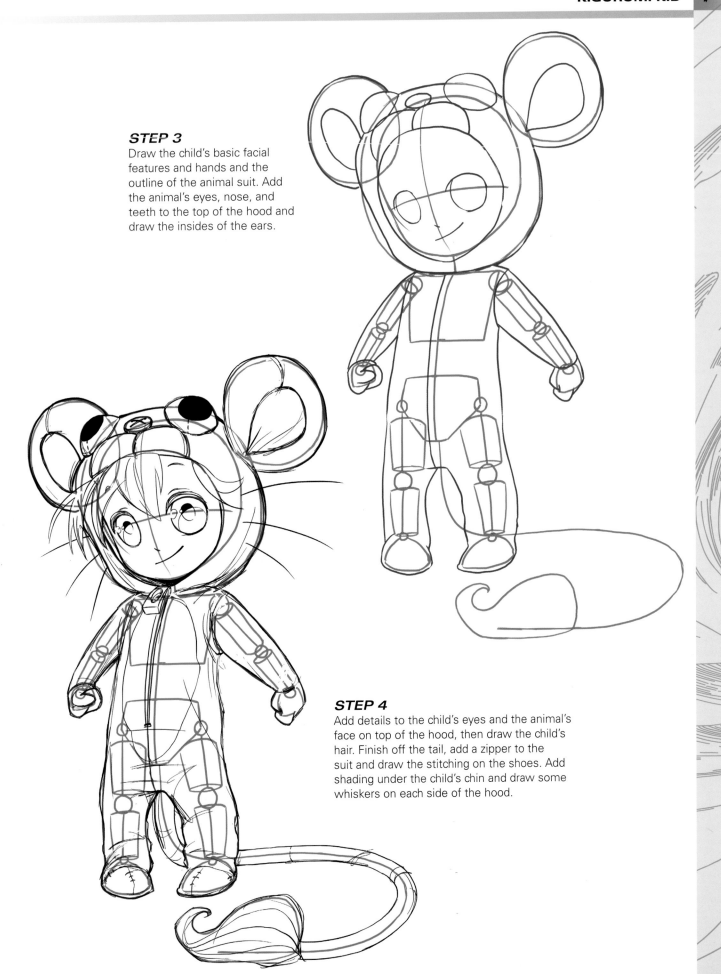

STEP 3
Draw the child's basic facial features and hands and the outline of the animal suit. Add the animal's eyes, nose, and teeth to the top of the hood and draw the insides of the ears.

STEP 4
Add details to the child's eyes and the animal's face on top of the hood, then draw the child's hair. Finish off the tail, add a zipper to the suit and draw the stitching on the shoes. Add shading under the child's chin and draw some whiskers on each side of the hood.

STEP 5
Use your lining pen to go over the lines that will be visible in the finished drawing, and erase any pencil lines.

STEP 6

Here's the character with the base color applied. Left like this the artwork could look very flat.

STEP 7
The subtle use of shadows wherever the material folds or gathers gives the drawing greater depth.

● ARTIST'S TIP
Using soft pastel colors will add to the overall cuteness of the picture. Brighter, more solid color choices would lose the innocence you are trying to capture with this character.

BUBBLEGUM GIRL

The first thing you notice about this character is her hair! Her head is very large compared to her body, but the artwork remains in balance. This is because we have added plenty of detail to her dress and thought carefully about the colors.

STEP 1
Draw a basic stick figure of a girl with a huge head, which is turned slightly to her left. Her arms are extended to her left-hand side and her hands are close together.

STEP 2
Use cylinder shapes to give form to her arms and lower legs and draw two lines marking the sides of her neck and the basic shapes for her hands. Now draw the girl's hair, which is tied up in bunches on either side of her head, and her flared, knee-length skirt.

STEP 3
Draw her basic shape, including her large, rounded eyes, button nose, and open mouth. Then draw her fingers, which are clasped together.

STEP 4
Add more detail to the girl's eyes and hair and draw the large bows and curling ribbons tying up her pigtails. Now draw her shoes and dress with its frills, bows, and long, puffed sleeves.

STEP 5

Use your lining pen to go over the lines that will be visible in the finished drawing, and erase any pencil lines. Draw the girl's upper lip and teeth and her thick black eyelashes. Color her pupils black. Now add the details to her dress and draw lines to show the gathers in her full skirt.

STEP 6
A pretty pale pastel shade has been used for the dress to give the character an extra dose of cuteness.

STEP 7
Shading is now added to the base colors. Notice the use of darker colors along the edges of the skirt on the side farthest from the light source, denoting the folds in the material.

GOTH GIRL

Creating a character like this goth girl allows you to keep a cute feel to your work while introducing a more serious storyline. This girl is making a statement with her clothes: she is quite capable of coping with life's gritty challenges.

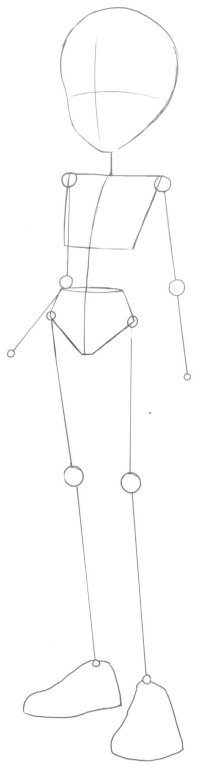

STEP 1
Draw a basic stick figure of a girl with a large head and long legs. Most of her right arm is hidden behind her body.

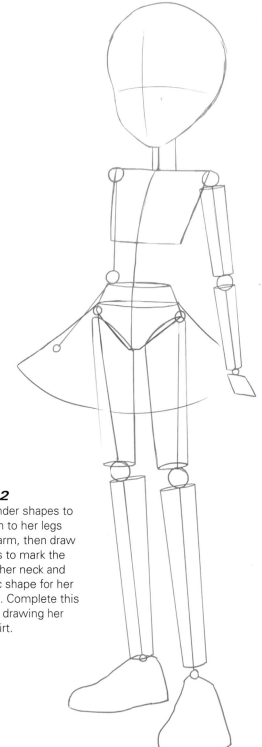

STEP 2
Use cylinder shapes to give form to her legs and left arm, then draw two lines to mark the sides of her neck and the basic shape for her left hand. Complete this stage by drawing her flared skirt.

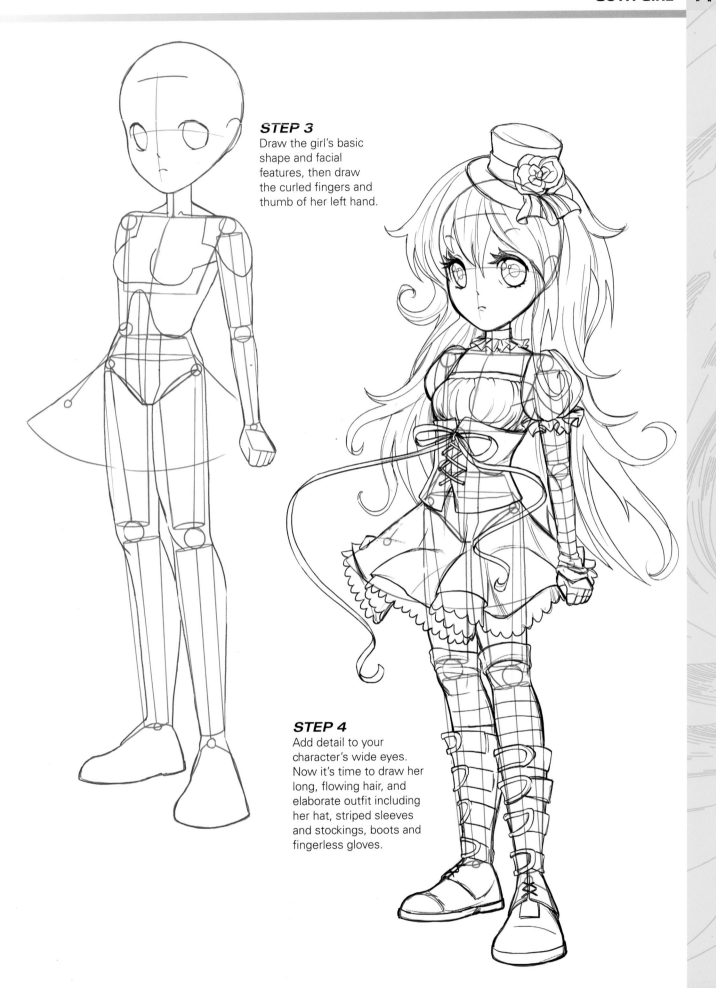

STEP 3
Draw the girl's basic shape and facial features, then draw the curled fingers and thumb of her left hand.

STEP 4
Add detail to your character's wide eyes. Now it's time to draw her long, flowing hair, and elaborate outfit including her hat, striped sleeves and stockings, boots and fingerless gloves.

STEP 5
Use your lining pen to go over the lines that will be visible in the finished drawing, and erase any pencil lines.

STEP 6
We used a very strong shade for her dress to ensure her outfit would not be completely upstaged by her hair color.

STEP 7

Pay close attention to the hair when adding shadows and highlights to ensure it is really given shape and definition. It is one of this character's most striking features, so spending the extra time is well worth it.

● ARTIST'S TIP

The face of your character is really important. As in real life, the face is the first place you look when connecting with another person. Here the pale skin framed by dark hair creates an area of high contrast that draws your eye to her face. The cool green of her eyes also helps them stand out against the warm reds and purples.

MINI MONSTER

What would manga and anime be without small, cute monsters? When it comes to designing them, try basing your monster's features on those of an existing animal and then exaggerating them. Let your imagination run wild!

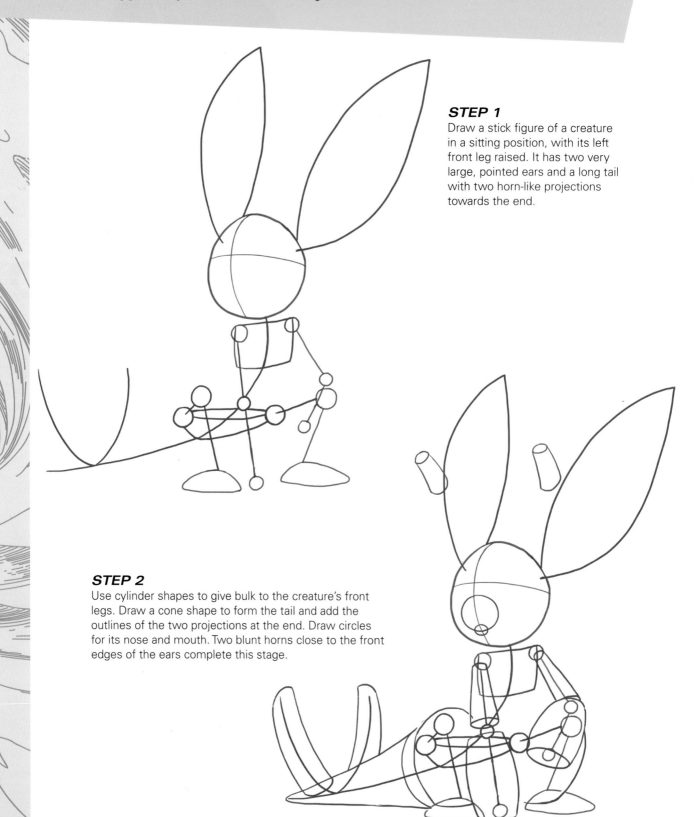

STEP 1
Draw a stick figure of a creature in a sitting position, with its left front leg raised. It has two very large, pointed ears and a long tail with two horn-like projections towards the end.

STEP 2
Use cylinder shapes to give bulk to the creature's front legs. Draw a cone shape to form the tail and add the outlines of the two projections at the end. Draw circles for its nose and mouth. Two blunt horns close to the front edges of the ears complete this stage.

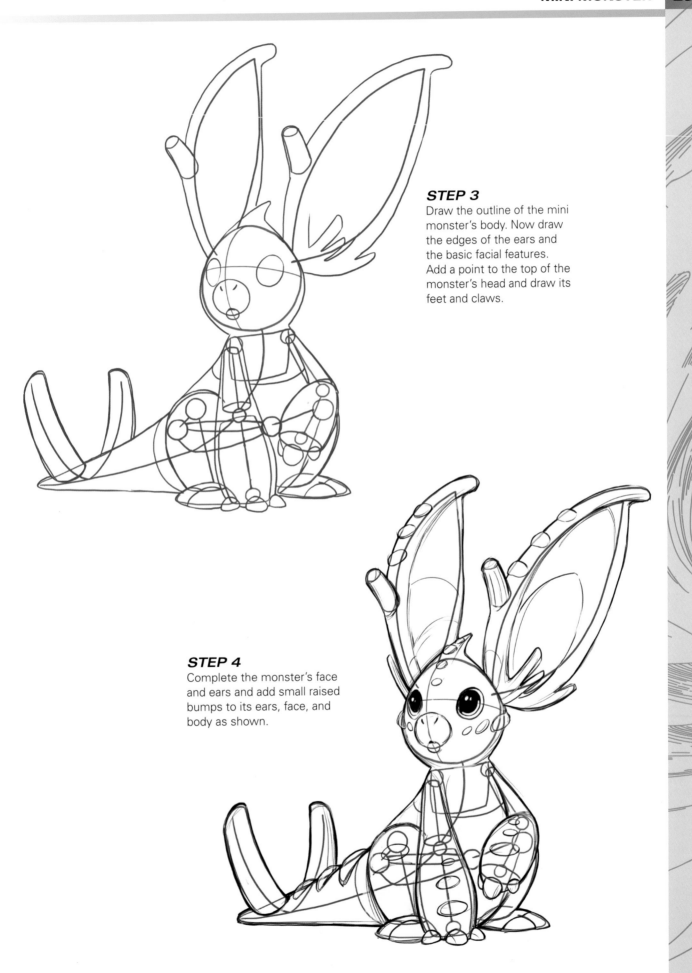

STEP 3

Draw the outline of the mini monster's body. Now draw the edges of the ears and the basic facial features. Add a point to the top of the monster's head and draw its feet and claws.

STEP 4

Complete the monster's face and ears and add small raised bumps to its ears, face, and body as shown.

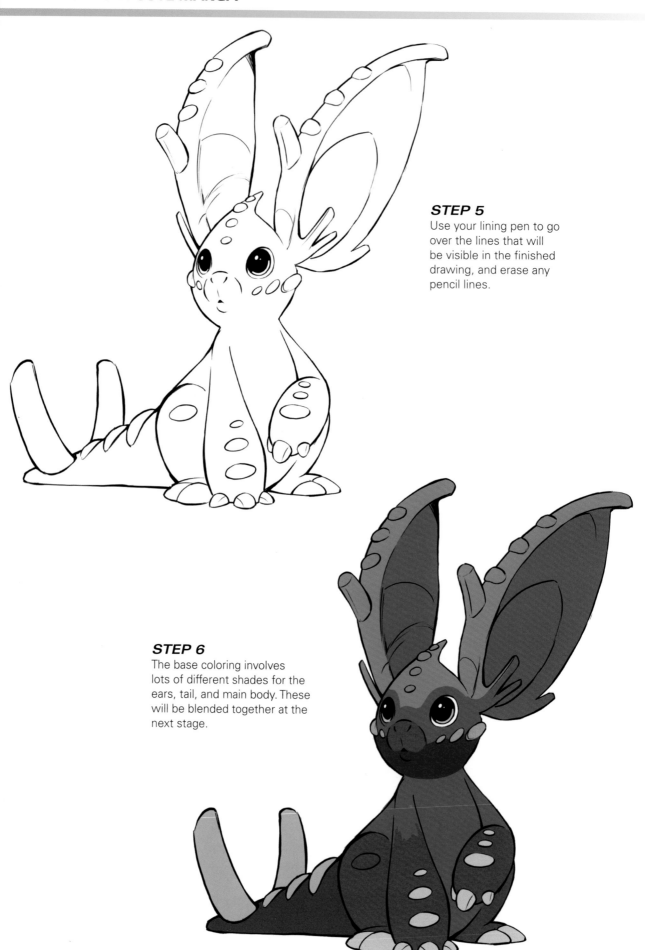

STEP 5
Use your lining pen to go over the lines that will be visible in the finished drawing, and erase any pencil lines.

STEP 6
The base coloring involves lots of different shades for the ears, tail, and main body. These will be blended together at the next stage.

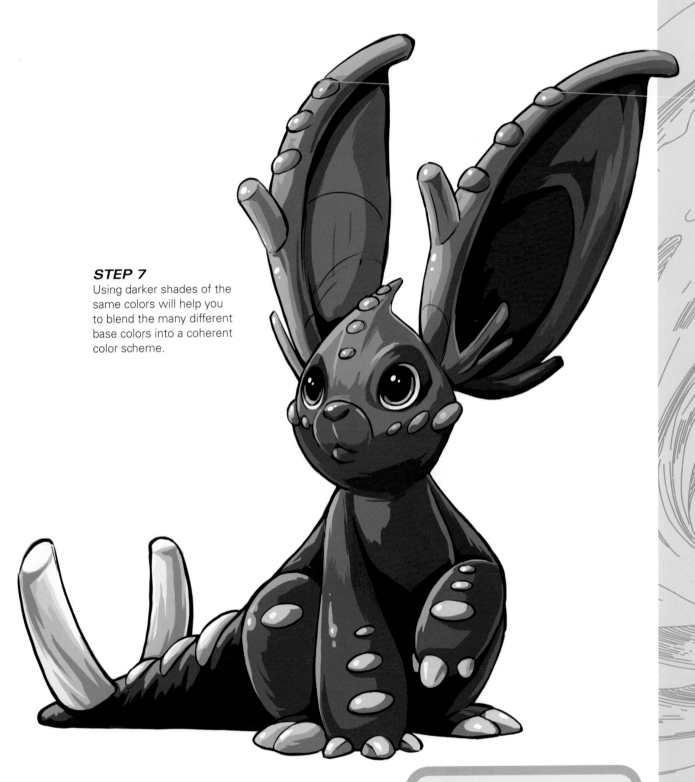

STEP 7
Using darker shades of the same colors will help you to blend the many different base colors into a coherent color scheme.

ARTIST'S TIP
Using several shades of the base colors creates an interesting and detailed effect. Don't forget to add highlights where light reflects the most. This will help to make the creature's ears and scales look shiny.

EXPRESSIVE EYES

The eyes play a major part in manga and many people will recognize a manga-style character from the eyes alone. The tips here show you how to position the eyes correctly and give you some techniques to make your eyes extra-expressive.

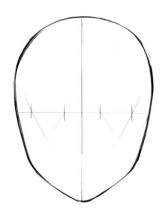

Creating eyes

Draw a basic face shape and divide it in half horizontally and vertically. Mark the outer and inner edges of the eyes along the horizontal line. Once you have the two marks for each eye, draw angled lines to form a V-shape below the eyes. Where these points cross will be the lower edge of the eyes.

Create curves above and below the horizontal line to mark out the upper and lower eyelashes. Add another pair of curves higher up for the eyebrows. Remember that the shape of the eyebrows can change depending on the expression you are drawing.

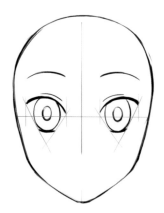

Draw a round shape between the two eyelashes to form the main part of the eye. Mimic a smaller version of the circle to form the pupil. Notice how the circles stay within your guidelines and how the eyelid overlaps the iris of the eye a little to give a relaxed look to the expression.

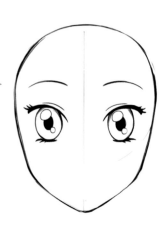

Draw smaller circles overlapping the pupils top and bottom and leave those white to show light bouncing off the surface of the eye. Thicken the lash lines and add a few upturned lines at the outer edge to show the lashes.

Leaving white space all the way around the iris will create a surprised or scared expression.

Shading the top part of the iris indicates the shadow created by the upper lid and lashes. It gives more depth to the eye.

Large pupils and irises combined with plenty of light reflections are a good way to make the eyes look cuter. This is typical of the chibi style of manga.

Happy characters close their eyes in manga drawings. A deep curve like this with a little flick at the end is the way to draw this expression. Combine it with a big grin for maximum effect.

Adding lots of little lines within the iris is an easy way to create more natural-looking eyes.

Bringing the inner edge of the eyebrow closer to the top of the eye will suggest a frown. Exaggerating the angle of the eyebrow will create an angry or calculating expression.

MISCHIEVOUS IMP

Not every character drawn in the chibi style has to be all sparkly and nice. How about a cute, fairy-like character with a mischievous personality? She can be just as dangerous to your heroes as a fire-breathing dragon.

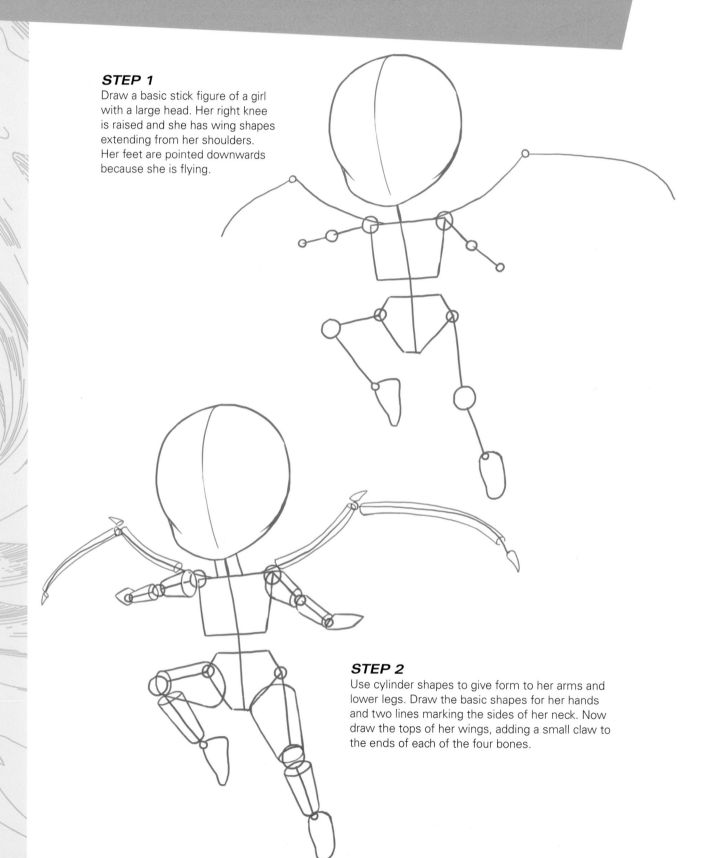

STEP 1

Draw a basic stick figure of a girl with a large head. Her right knee is raised and she has wing shapes extending from her shoulders. Her feet are pointed downwards because she is flying.

STEP 2

Use cylinder shapes to give form to her arms and lower legs. Draw the basic shapes for her hands and two lines marking the sides of her neck. Now draw the tops of her wings, adding a small claw to the ends of each of the four bones.

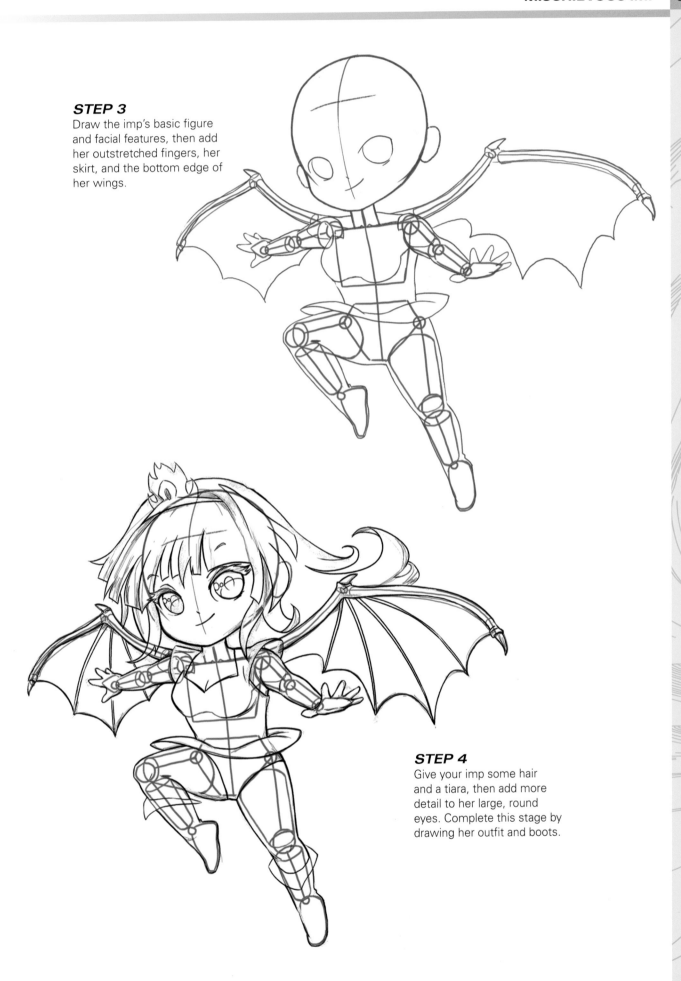

STEP 3
Draw the imp's basic figure and facial features, then add her outstretched fingers, her skirt, and the bottom edge of her wings.

STEP 4
Give your imp some hair and a tiara, then add more detail to her large, round eyes. Complete this stage by drawing her outfit and boots.

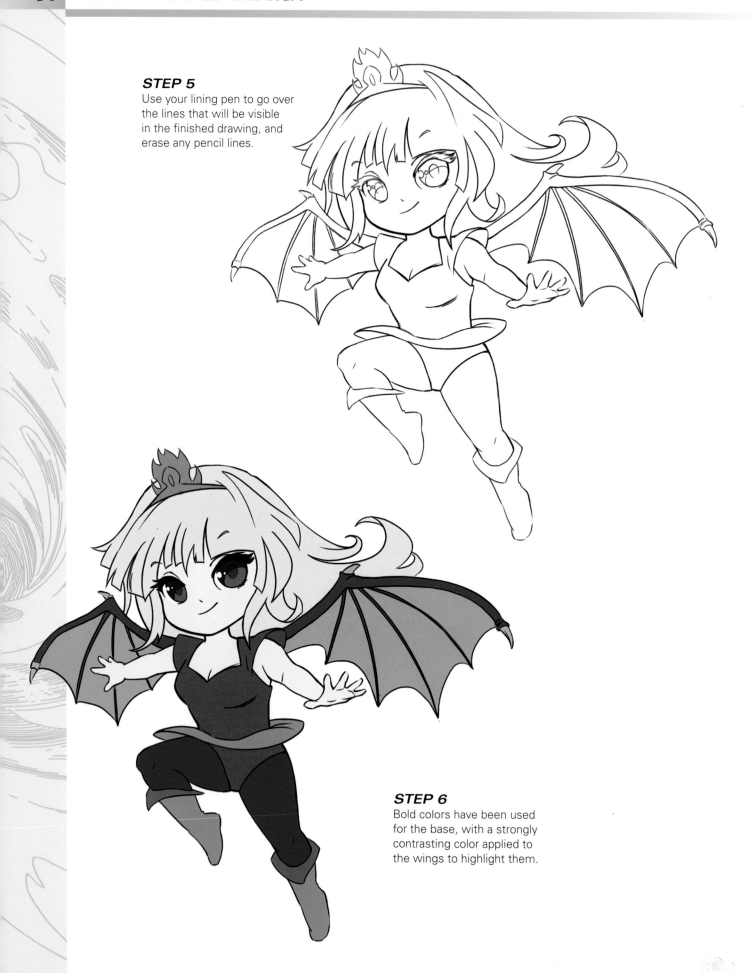

STEP 5
Use your lining pen to go over the lines that will be visible in the finished drawing, and erase any pencil lines.

STEP 6
Bold colors have been used for the base, with a strongly contrasting color applied to the wings to highlight them.

STEP 7
Darker colors are used for the shading. Note that all-important manga sparkle in her eyes.

GLOSSARY

accessories Things that are worn or carried to match an outfit. This can be bags, hats, shoes, gloves, jewelry, hairbands, and other items.

anime A style of animation which began in Japan.

chibis Small versions of manga characters, with big heads and exaggerated expressions.

fairy A small magical creature, often with wings.

goth A style of fashion. Goths typically wear dark clothes, often with elements of Victorian dress.

gritty Showing the unpleasant side of life as it really is.

imp A small magical character, with a naughty personality.

innocence Being pure, simple, and harmless.

kigurumi The Japanese word for people who dress up in an animal costume.

mischievous Playfully annoying or causing harm.

pastels Soft, delicate colors.

tiara A small crown.

FURTHER READING

How to Draw Manga Chibis & Cute Critters by Samantha Whitten (Walter Foster, 2012)

Ready, Set, Draw!: Manga by Ailin Chambers (Gareth Stevens, 2014)

Write and Draw Your Own Comics by Louie Stowell (Usborne, 2014)

WEBSITES

Due to the changing nature of Internet links, PowerKids Press has developed an online list of websites related to the subject of this book. This site is updated regularly. Please use this link to access the list: **www.powerkidslinks.com/um/cute**

INDEX